Desire My Dream Poetry

𝒥B
Juanita Betts

*J*B
Desire My Dream Productions

For information regarding distribution, promotional and/or
marketing services, Lulu Inc.
functions as agent at Lulu.com

Manufactured in the United States of America.
Updated version – January 2010
First Edition October 2007

ISBN: 978-0-6151-7156-2

Dedication

Dedicated to My Mother, My Sisters,
My Baby Girl Timia,
My extended Family, and close Friends.
You all BELIEVED in me and I will LOVE you forever!

Acknowledgments

Giving thanks to my family, and my daughter Timia Baez the best gift ever that was gave to me, besides life. I Love you Baby Girl! In addition, I give Thanks to all. I have loved in my life for various reasons and have educated and inspired me to write this book through out time. One should know that Love is a very strong emotion, which changes you in various ways, and move you into different directions.

All my life I have made an effort to treat people with respect, and loyalty. If for any reason I have not done so, please forgive me for I did not mean to treat you so. However, for the ones I have treated as I would have wanted to be treated, and you did the vice versa to me. I forgive you with all of my being, and hope your life is blessed.

Thank you God for the Gift of Writing!

Points of a Star

Love
Pain
Strength
Dreams
Life

Desire is for our Dreams

1
Love

Mental Love Making

Have you ever had someone make love to your mental, before

the physical?

It is an appreciative experience

It is a glorifying experience that makes you say

'Dam, when did this happen, or how this happen'

We started out as friends, and have become more than friends

First I didn't feel I was ready, but then I said to myself

Why not, give it a try because his words and actions are

All so sweet and melting the ice

Breaking down barriers of fright of past and present pain

I come to repair and protect your heart

A man who knows what he wants

A man who knows special without touching physically

Because lust and love can be mistaken

Have you ever had someone make love to your mental, before

the physical?

No insecurities should I bear

Because he appreciates me

He is considerate of my feelings

And he listens to me

Wants me totally not part of me

We click; we have so much in common

On the same page and willing to build

A strong foundation of love and honesty

Loyalty is hard to find, Love is hard to find

I have so much love inside but next time will only

Give to another who appreciates it

Someone who is worthy of it

Because it is too special to waste my time

Have you ever had someone make love to your mental, before

the physical?

'I have'

And it is an amazing feeling to have and share for a life time

and grow old together he says

I thank God I have found you or did we find each other

Doesn't matter because I feel we were meant to be

And that God possibly put us in each other path

So what God has put together let no man tear apart

He is making love to my mental

How do you handle that?

Acceptance

Willingness

Openness

To what he has to offer

Because it's worth it and I am worthy

And so is He, because he made love to my mental first

And that Heals the Heart

Finder's Keepers

When someone loves you

They treasure you

Treasure is to hold on to, and desired

If you are no longer with your love, then you were not his

treasure

His eyes were, *closed*

But there is always another

With his eyes wide, open

Realizing this gold does glitter

He is polishing it off to a shine

He did not have to chase

You threw her away

Not realizing your own treasure

And he says

"Found treasure is a gift, gifts you always keep"

You...

So gentle but hard

So loving but strong

So humble but humorous

So decent but rugged

So intelligent but witty

So artistic but laid back

You...

I like

I desire

I want

I have

and I am so content

To trade for anything else would be

Unthinkable at this point

so for You...

I am Happy!

Friends

When I needed someone to talk to, you were there

When I needed someone to just listen to me, you were there

When I needed advice, you were there

When I needed some hard love, you were there

When I needed a kick in my ass

You were there

Mostly when I needed your support, you gave me your hand

The gift was your love and respect

That gift will last forever

While we are miles apart, know I am still there

I understand that and hope you do too

Although we may not speak on a regular

Or see each other as usual, does not mean any of the above is

gone

Because the love and respect I have for my true friends will

never die

Even when I take my last breath

Remember who was real, there for you and there for me

I am that real ride or die chic in all aspects

Please never forget that because

I am your Friend for Life!

Living

I met this guy and I want to get to know him

I am excited yet unsure of what I might do

to possibly mess it up before it gets started

because of recent past pain

Not trying to punish him for another *man* erroneous ways

that wouldn't be fair, but I know I am not an angel

and neither is he

so do I go with the flow

just live for the day

and not think or worry about

what HAS happened...

The past is just that

so leave it there, right?

yeah that's what I'll do

because I want to get to know the brother

I owe him a fair chance

as well as myself, a fair chance

He may just be the one made just for me

Rhythm

You touch me and I moan

You kiss me and I groan

You enter me and I sigh

I touch you and you look at me

The rhythm is so right

You say um hum

I say oh yes

Our bodies clash and we mash

Such a beautiful design

Two bodies colliding in delight

In the heat of the moment

Its hot, you can barely breathe

The air is so thick

Then you release with a sigh of relief

When our bodies collide in our rhythm

No other can match

Because I know what you like

Delectable

Its 7 pm, a decent hour to begin

I wonder if you are coming over

To give me that delectable sound you always make me moan

You come in you smile

We talk and I look at you as if to say

Shut up and just take off your clothes

But I say nothing, just look and desire all that I want to taste...

Eventually not rushing

I sense you wanting me...more than earlier

The animal instinct is prominent

The lust is desirable

I look at you as if you are a lion and you look at me as if I am a

lioness

Protecting me for your feast for the night

I groan, I moan because I am the kingdom

Waiting for the king to enter my dome

Wow, this feels so good, so delectable, so enchanting

So wet

I want you; you want me, so we delve into the sensation of lust

and desire

All over the kitchen counter, the floor, the staircase

Ooooohhhh

We all over

You taste me, so much like sweet nectar of peaches

and don't let go until you hear and see me climb the wall

Understand my brotha, once I climb that wall

I am ready to ride you ...

So if you packing my brotha let me ride

Ride it like a stallion....

A Black Mandingo- ess stallion

Soul Love

When I met you, I knew that you were for me

Even though you did not want, what I wanted, but it felt right

You say we never clicked the way you thought or wished

However, to me I saw us click on numerous occasions

What did you not feel?

Was I too aggressive or was I just not, what you desired

Oh, when we made love our souls met

I know you felt it because you were always satisfied

This I know because you never wanted to leave me

Oh, what went wrong?

Dam this hurts so badly

Something only God, time or you can heal

What to do

Do I sit and wait

Continue to pray for strength

Hope that one day I will hear you call my name

Give me that heart felt hug that you always gave

So many feelings inside that felt outside

Feeling of you inside my soul was the most beautiful thing that

I have ever felt in my life, where only God dwelled

People say oh girl you deserve better, but I say I want you!

How do I get pass this pain when I allowed you into my soul

It is hard to release something from your soul

The love I feel inside for you is amazing

Why you do not want it

Why not embrace it and feel loved by an angel

Flaw of Love

I let you into my soul

Only because I felt you were right

God is the only man I should have in my soul

Unless I know, you are right for me

I allowed myself to fall victim to love a man way past

What my heart can offer, or should not offer

Without gaining the same

Is that wrong, was that wrong

I do not know

I ask for forgiveness if I was wrong

I ask for understanding if IT was wrong

We are only flesh and blood

All looking for some type of love

But a good love in many different forms

The love I am looking for is an unconditional love

A grateful love

Appreciative love

A Respectful and Desirable love

Where is that Urban Renaissance Man?

If there is such a thing

The brother that knows what he wants

Because here is a sister who know hers

My BF

Ever had someone you could tell your hopes and dreams to

I feel like I lost that friend who I was able to do that

Just lay back and talk about any type of ish

You ever had a friend like that

We use to laugh, watch movies, and hang out

Do that nasty ish and was oh sweet

Now I have no one to do those things with

That has some meaning

It just feels so much better when there is meaning

Because I know you, and you know me

This makes it better than trying to prove who you are

Because I don't know you just yet

Is not how I want it to be just yet?

However, it is out of my hands

Dam this is sad

I feel like I lost my **Best Friend** today

You & I

Before I met you, I was alone with no real solution to my
loneliness, as it seemed
However, I was looking within myself to see what I wanted
My flaws attempt to fix them, so...
At the time I really did not care or was reaching for it, but was
willing to attempt it again from what I had learned of myself
Not just with *anyone*, but with someone of purpose in life and
a goal
Now that you are in my life for just a minute so far, I have
come to the first phase of love for you as the person you are
which is a *beautiful* person
I have *much* more room for the love to grow, which is another
beautiful thing and I want to attempt it with you
You are a sensual man, a loving man, and a man that knows
what he wants in a woman, whether it's from experience or
just knowing
You are at this moment in time, the man I want to share my
life with in all ways

I want to learn you, know you, live you, and be with you

I want to love you, respect you, need you, desire you and adore
you....

I want to be a part of you, a partner with you, your lover friend
and your freak....

I want to face problems together and grow, be there for you at
all times in good and bad

Be centered so really listen

I am willing to do and learn new things to keep it harmonized

I want to be able to share and grow as an individual and as a

team... I don't want to hurt you, I would never cheat on you

never steal from you, all I want to do is love you...and *all* that
comes with you...

Will you continue to let me... show you my love?

I am *not* your past; and neither *you* mine I am your present
and your future, if you *allow* me to be...

Sorry for your pain, but I want to be your gain as you mine

Will you allow, and open your heart completely to me; can you
trust your heart to me?

I would like to love your heart and massage it back into a

whole piece, because it is fragile, and needs caressing

Caressing of real love, loyalty and trust, can I?

We can move *slowly, slowly together*, and it will be all right

just trust me, love me, respect me and you will feel the

difference

Black Love

I know it may seem a little extreme right now

Like I am crazy

I am actually trying to understand you

Trying to believe and trust you

Hoping you are able to talk to me

Let me know what is good

Protect me since it is only about me

Why protect others if they suppose not to exist

It is not all my fault

We are at each other's throat right now

Or just not talking

I thought this could possibly be my time

Now I do not know

If it is my time

Maybe I am not what you want

Maybe you are not what I want

Maybe we just being tested right now

To see if we can handle this black love baby

You know how it is

You tell me what's good

Therefore, I can protect myself

Just in case you slip

I need to be on point at all times can't you see

Then I can handle myself a lot better to

Not stress you over this *bullshit*

Sweet Second's Love

You hurt him

You betrayed him

You did not believe in him

Do you know what you did?

You made it harder for me

Why is that?

Not that you were bad for him

Why do this if you loved him

It is ok, because even though you made

It harder for me

It is ok

Because I will make it harder for you

To even attempt to get him back

Because you will attempt but

It is ok

Because I know, I have not

Betrayed him

I know I did not hurt him

I know I believed in him

He knows that I love him

Ask me why I did that

Well, because he loves me

Let me come in

I want to treat my man like a king

How can I?

When my king will not let me in

It makes me wonder, is there another

Is it the same other that he once let come in

This was not me unfortunately

When he is not with me, I wonder could there still be another

Thoughts flow through your mind

Come home My King and let me come in

Taste my love, your one and only Queen

This Love

Your eyes are like diamonds

They glow when you look at me

Your smile is like the moon

Glowing in the night

O' such a wonderful sight

When you make love to me

It's like your favorite meal or dessert

You want to savor it forever

Your love is so sweet and oh so different

I will try to hang in there

To endure

I really do not know how

Help me to love the type of loving you are giving

Respectful Love

When you love someone

It should be a respectful love

Letting your partner know

Certain things that is important

When you don't respect the one you love

You do whatever you want

When you want without letting your partner

Know anything

That sort of love you can keep

I do not *want* it

My Man

I love my man, I really do

when he is not with me I desire him even more

When he is not feeling me, I desire him even more

I want to be there for him the way a woman should

but some men are afraid to let you

totally come in, why? I ask

past relationships most of all

but I am not that person, and you are with me NOW!

I love my man, want to be his backbone

want to be his lover, want to be his freak

and want to be his friend

Come to me my man, let me show you

how it feels to love and treated, as a King

but you have to let me come in

to feel my love, love of a QUEEN

This Guy

There is a guy, who stands alone

Roving the streets on a daily basis

Not acknowledging what he has at home

Never to be where he should be

Always stands alone

Talking is not his best asset, asking is not either

I still love that guy

Who stands alone

Today I wonder will it be different

Today it is not

Nothing is what I gather from his behalf

Where he stands alone

Take me in your arms

Just hold me for a moment

Not too much to ask, is it?

Please, stop standing alone

I Promise

I promise I will love you

Respect you

Appreciate you

Consider you

Be loyal to you

Therefore, you can trust me

I promise I will satisfy you

Therefore, you do not want

Need

Desire the next one

I promise I will be Loyal to you

Therefore, you will not have to wonder

Be insecure

Ponder if I am late

I promise I will be by your side

When the times are rough

Times are good

Times are harder than rough

As long as I know, you love me

Have the security that all will be fine

I promise to need you

I promise to want you

I promise, do you hear me

Are you listening?

I can promise you all these things

I promise

We

Am I the one for you?

Are you the one for me?

We both do not know

However, can we just see?

Is the past holding you back?

Is the past holding we back?

I am not sure

I know who I am

In addition, who you are, and we are different

So just let us be

Let us see

What we can do

As this we

Royal Love

The jewels on her crown

The stars in her eyes

Confidence and sincerity is all

About her face when she is with him

The feeling she gets from being with him

Is of royalty, true royalty

I am a queen when I am with you

You are my king

So gentle, so real

A feeling I have never felt before

Is new to me

Is this the feeling of true love?

Is this a dream?

For if it is

Do not awake me

Loving you

When you talk to me, I feel your benevolence

Your softness of masculinity

When you hold me, it feels warm

I feel safe; I feel secure

When you kiss me, I feel a warm softness

With a profuse, desire of passion

When you make love to me, I want to say

How you make me feel, but the words are tedious

Therefore, you leave me speechless

Not knowing what to say

Except an enchanting abundance

Of delectable soft sounds

So I just bask myself in the delightful

Satisfying feeling, you leave me with

Wanting more and more

This brings me closer to you, therefore

I have no reason to lose my way

Because you are all I ever needed in my life

You are my dream man

Which I have been yearning

Did not know how to locate you

We found each other on a cordial October night

Since then the indicator been fixed on green

At a traffic light

I do not want to stop

I do not want to crash

I just want to keep going

See how exquisite our love can truly be

2
Pain

Waiting is a Virtue

When I asked, would you wait for me?

You said yes!

Once you were gone it became a mess

You changed and rearranged our plans

Once you were at your destination

You decided another task

You saw other possibilities, so you thought

Running and ripping doing things I would hope not

Lies were told, games were played

Decisions made that did not include me

What was there to gain?

Nothing but change, a new life he said

New life without me how could that be if you love me?

I said I was coming to be with you we made plans

Now you have more than expected

Greener grass so he thought more like empty pockets

Because now your new life

Involves a new life into this world

Because you didn't think of me

You were selfish

Believing Love

Love believes

Love is sharing

Love is trusting

Love is having your back, even when I don't have my own

Love is having your back, when you are not strong to have

your own

Love is being there when the other is not

Love wants you

Love needs you

Love desires only you

Love, what is Love?

Love is caring about the others feelings

Decisions, and your actions show if you love me or not

So, do you love me?

I Fucked Up!

I lied to you

I stole from you

I treated you like you were a skank

Even though you had more class than any chic

I ever been with

I didn't believe you

Even though you were that chic who handled her shit

I fucked up!

I did things because you were not here by my side

I thought you were doing you

Even when you were only feeling me

I didn't trust you

Should have been a stronger man to know that you loved me

Just for me and not what I had

Now I did the UNTHINKABLE with another

Even though I knew, you loved me

I continued to hurt you

I fucked up!

Stupid decisions

Stupid actions

All my fault because I didn't believe you when I should have

Once Again, He fucked up!

The Flip Side

Hurt me to love another

Now you want me

But afraid to hurt her

The way you hurt me

What is that?

So confusing

Be true to thyself

You lied under false pretences to get with her

You said to her

That you did not want me

A lie

That you did not desire me

A lie

That it was over with us

A lie

You pushed me away, which was *not* your intention

It moved so fast you said, *which* is not like you

What were you actually trying to do?

He says

Get to know her

Get her to trust me

Get her to open up

This *now* hurts you, to know how much you hurt me

Now you want, desire and miss what we had

But afraid to hurt again

So unhappy you stay until you free yourself

Be true to thyself

You never hurt one to get with another

Based on a lie

Eventually there will be a flipside

Is it all worth the pain for which you *know* and *love*?

For another, you *do not* really know or love

Still a stranger

When I first met you, you treated me as if I was an angel

Now being treated as a stranger

Isn't it suppose to grow

Why is it below what it was instead of greater than?

Not suppose to be that way

Ask what about me you do not like

You say I have not done anything you do not like

So what's up with this picture?

The past he says

I am not that one who hurt you

Let my love in

Been trying to show you my love

Therefore, you could see that I am not HER

However, you will not let me unlock that broken heart

So how can you really feel my love?

The Right One

Are you the right one to give my heart?

Tried this few times before, still has not worked

My heart cannot take any more pain

I cannot cry anymore do you know this

Too many tears I have shared

For what

For who

I cannot cry anymore do you know this

Wonder if this means I do not care

I cannot love

I just have a barrier over my heart

Do you have what it takes to break that barrier?

It is not made of steel, its breakable like glass

I can see through and this is why I see you

So I am asking again are you the right one to give my heart to

Fatal Reactions

Reactions of love can be so strong that you can

Bite your own tongue off with the harsh things

That we say, I know my tongue is sharp

Sometimes too sharp

I try not to be this way

But I am a bull when provoked I attack

Do not like to be this way

However, this is what I am and who I am...

I try to fight it back so many times

Always find myself in situations as such

It is all love it is not pain

That I want to bring to you

My sweet baby boy, man of the day

Please understand that I am human just like you

Liable to make a mistake or two

Just hold me and tell me it will be all right

No matter what others may try to say or fight

All I need is a kiss on the neck and a whisper

It will be all right

Then it will soften me and I will know all is ok

Instead, I get nothing so alone I stay

Thought you loved me

My friend called me and said today

My man hit me, and beat me in my face

She cried, but he loves me he said

I said to her, how that could be

A fist in the face is no sign of love for me

She said, he told me he loved me

I said to her, was this before he hit your face?

No after she said, I said to her

If it was before

He would have never hit your face

Deceiving

I once had a man who loved me to death

I thought from the treatment I received

Each day I got flowers, kisses, dinners and gifts

However, some nights I was beaten

And couldn't figure out his trick

I asked, and I asked why you do this?

He said to me, because...

You are mine

I said to him

I belong to no one

No one but God and thyself

So please stop hitting me

Today

Today is a day I feel alone

No one to talk to

No one to hold me, to say

"Hey, let's do something"

It is a harsh feeling that you feel in your heart

Even more so when you have someone

That does not spend that special time with you

For what ever reason

It is a hurting feeling

Wanting and desiring to be with someone

Who will not let you?

Today I feel alone

Emptiness of love

A feeling of a deep desire

A desire to love

Reaching out to someone to touch you

To be with you

It feels like a big hole

An empty hole waiting to fill

With a mere hug

Or a soft word of affection

One fails to understand

Emptiness of love is loneliness

One, which makes the heart hard and cold

Why keep a delicate flower that needs water

EMPTY to wilt from a drought

This feeling

When you are near me

I do not know how to feel

I know I love you

Love is not enough

For how I feel when I see you

So what is this feeling?

I ask myself

Is it love or am I falling out of love

Hmmm I wonder

What is this empty feeling?

When I see you

Fading Love

Where did the passion go?

It use to be so nice

We use to hold each other so tight

Look into each other eyes and smile

I LOVE YOU

Now its quiet, no smiles, just frowns

As if, you no longer want us to be a tomorrow

No passion, no fire, let alone desire

Where did it go, what happened?

Did we just take it all for granted and sit and

Watch it disappear, or is there still hope

Do we work on it?

Do we let it go to see if there is another?

For you and for me

Selfish, Not you

Why do you use my stuff?

Why do you touch my stuff?

Why, Why, Why

If I am your girl

Then why can I not use or touch your stuff

I share with you, on a daily basis

You use my car, my phone, and you eat my food

You sleep in my bed too

Why do I have to ask?

When, I always share with you

Wondering

I wonder what you are thinking

I sit and look at you, and I wonder

Am I on your mind is she on your mind

I see you smile, I see you frown

I see you in deep thought

Oh, which one was for me?

The smile or the frown, I do not know

I wonder

Could it be a thought of neither?

My Precious Heart

Have you ever felt like your heart was bleeding?

Try loving someone so much in fear of losing them twice

It is a feeling, a painful feeling

Desirable feeling that is unbelievable

Have you ever cried yourself to sleep hoping for some

honesty?

Do you really love me?

You say that you do

Because dam baby, I love you

It's unbelievable the love I have inside for you

I just want to scream or take my own heart out and

Caress it back to health

Help me breath

Resuscitate me

You're not responsible

You say you are not responsible

but you sleep in my bed

You say you are not responsible

but you eat in my kitchen

You say you are not responsible

but I wash your clothes

You say you are not responsible

but you have used space in my house

You say you are not responsible to help me pay rent

you say it is my responsibility

so I guess its okay for your child to be on the street

Home should come first, no matter what you want to do

because you do have a responsibility

not only meaning what *you* may think it means

because you are responsible too

Yes I am

Once you said to me that

your friends were more responsible than I was

Your friend's do more for you than I but you live in my house

how can that be?

Oh, your friends are more responsible than I am

they don't take care of our child

But your friends are more responsible than me

you say if your friends needed you

you will be there

because they are there for you

for I have been by your side for years

lived in the same house

taking care responsibilities the best I saw fit

but I am not responsible

Yes, I have failed with some of my responsibilities

some point in time

but when I needed you

you came through but with an attitude

and did not understand why?

Because you said your friends were more responsible

but I am your woman

so why have the attitude

for if you were more responsible

I may have not failed at some point

of *our* responsibilities

3
Strength

Checkmate

No more games do I want to play

Are you still playing with the little pawn trying to get across

the board?

Are you still playing hangman trying to complete the hang?

Am I the one being hung out to dry?

Because you felt you had control of the ropes?

You were suppose to help me down from the ropes

You were suppose to be like the Bishop and the Knightsman to

Protect, trust and believe me, us, the we

Instead, you hung me out to dry

The games are over; I am the winner of this game

So guess what...

Checkmate!

Deserving

Loving you was like a new start for me, so I thought

I bent over backwards for you, even in tough times

Feeling as if you took me for granted, and now it's the end

Deserve this I ask myself, and the answer is always NO

Why would you treat your suppose to be Queen, as such

So mischievous were you, so mysterious you were

So secretive with lies always had another agenda

To live like that, so not cool

Learn to respect women on a higher level

Especially, the ones that are there for you like your mom

And your daughter, because I was there for you

just as they were

And look what I got in the end

Deserve this I ask myself, and the answer is always NO

Love; oh do you know what love really is about

Trust, do you really understand trust

Belief, you need to learn *how* to believe the ones that have

your best interest at HEART

Desire, learn to desire the only one you love

Love; oh do you know what love really is about

Deserve this I ask myself, and the answer is always NO

My Level

Age has nothing to do with being on my level

Let me explain...

Can you hold a conversation without misunderstanding?

Can you understand all that we speak on without explanation?

Can you listen to me and not be selfish?

By not wanting me to only, hear you

Can we say what's on our minds without playing games?

Instead of saying, what you think I want to hear?

Are you a boy or a man? Because I am a woman not a girl

Can you be truthful and really feel me?

Can you be acceptive and make me feel secure?

Are you a man or a boy? I am a woman not a girl

If I want to build with you would you be reckless and knock

down the Walls

or would you make sure the foundation is strong

so it could withstand the toughest storms

Would you respect my feelings as I respect yours?

Are you on my level?

Because I am a grown ass woman who know what she wants

Do you? Or are you still a boy

I Need You

Life takes you through some changes sometimes

make you sit and think about your life...

Let me say something to you right now

Are you listening to me...

I need your full attention...

God I need you right now

The devil is really trying to mess with my heart right now

I know you God, I know it seems like I am not there

But I am here God

Here my plea O' Lord!

I try to live right; I try to live by your rules

But the world is so COLD O' Lord

I need your Guidance O' Lord

I am tired O' Lord

Tired of the games, the lies

Tired of the world the way it is

O' Lord

I need some solace

I need some understanding

I need you to help me understand

O' Lord

I need you!

Am I in a Jar?

Am I in a jar, is the lid shut tight?

Am I walking around breathing air?

Hard to *discriminate* between the two

Feel like I am suffocating

Can someone loosen the lid?

Can I just cut a hole in the jar?

But with what tools

I have no tools inside

Outside I have *some* tools

When I am in this jar

The lid is so tight

I cannot reach my tools

Why are you trying to suffocate me?

When all I want to do is breath

Use my tools to succeed

Hold me *back* for what, my persona, my color

Just because

Loosen the lid and let me succeed

Let me breath

Because I will not change

I will always stand tall

Trust

Trust loves someone enough

To give your heart to

Bring them into your soul

But when damaged

Trust is hard to regain

It's a rarity to regain and when betrayed

It has gone forever

Trust is not a toy

But a cherished treasure

You pamper it

You feed it

You love it

Then maybe you will have that sacred base called trust, forever

Survival

Dreams are the foundation to survival

Love is the foundation of survival

Strength is the foundation in survival

Dreams are something that keeps us alive

Love is something that brings hope

Strength is the harvest, which grows within us to keep us alive

Although some may try to say, my dreams are nightmares

Although some may say that, my love is not real

No one can say that my strength is weak

Because I know that, I am a survivor

The Fight

I fight for who I am every day

I strive for better every day

I put on a face everyday

Don't want to put on a face everyday but

In this world, you have to at certain times of the day

I am not a fake or a hypocrite

But to survive for me and my kid

I will put on that face

Bite my tongue

Have some etiquette

To get my funds

I fight for who I am every day

But I will not kiss you know what

No, Not me on any given day

Therefore, I fight for who I am every day

You think so . . .

You think I am weak because I am female

Do you think I am weak because I am black?

Which is it?

To be honest you are weak for thinking that

Idiotic, Ignorant

Feministic, Prejudice

Stupid mess

I am smart because I am

I strive for greatness

Do not mistake me for a stereotype

It is not sufficient

Because I am an individual

And in my own class

Not better than the next

So do not get it twisted

I said, in my *own* class

My Word

Sometime in your life

You have to say to yourself

What am I doing?

What am I doing to myself?

A person can only do to you

As much as you let them

Sometime in your life, you have to wake up and say to yourself

No more, no more but there is only one catch

You have to *mean* it

Hold firm to your *OWN* word

Just do it

I have to work to make it

I have been working

I want to go to school to make it better

I am in school

I need a second job to make it easier

I will get that second job

I want to make my life more challenging

All it takes is a why, a how and an action

To make it better

My why, my daughter

My how, as I explained above

My action

I am *going* to do it

I *am* doing it

No more, want to

Just do it

Me

I will survive on my own

I do not need you

I will get my life together

I do not need you

I will get back on top

I do not need you

I will survive on my own

Do not make it seem as if

I need you

For life is my own

I will survive it, on my own

Don't worry

I use to sit and worry about where you were

I use to sit and worry about what you were doing

Whom you were with

I use to sit and beat myself up

Cry and cry until I realized

I was crying for nothing

For when you came in from hanging

Out all night I should have known

My questions would not hold a bite

Answers received were not suffice

It was bland and shallow

Oh what a shame

I should have known

I should have never sat and worried

And lost sleep for this shit

So why worry...

Fatal choice to live

I struggled and struggled

Felt I was losing

Kept struggling and struggling

Please let me go, please stop

"NO, can't do that, I'm not finished yet"!

Was all he kept saying...

Unfortunately, to say I gave up struggling for the fear of my

life

So he could finish

However, my life was in danger and *fear* in my heart

I would rather him take *my* **treasures**

Than take my life

Reason or Season

You came back into my life

Whether if it's for a reason or a season

I just want to thank you

For reversing my frown into a smile

Something that was misplaced

Because my past was a mess

However, right now, you are a part of my life

Whichever part that is

It is making me feel vibrant

Vibrant once again

Our roots are similar and that brings excitement

Our bodies connect and that brings pleasure

Our intellect is real and that brings harmony

You, I thank you for coming back into my life

You are a good and decent man

Just wanted you to know that just incase no one

Have told you that lately

I am giving you that today

I thank you once again for coming back into my life

Whether if it's for a reason or a season

I am enjoying and loving each moment in time

Sweet 16

At 16, high school sweetheart so much in love

He left one day to another city leaving me all alone

Feeling real down, I cried and cried

At 16, my close friend died one night

After a football game

I remember that day *so* vividly

In class with a headache, go home I said

No I'll be alright he said

But he left us

At 16, I took some pills, and tried to take my life

No doubt

But thank god, I did not succeed...

Because my life would been wasted for nothing

You see

Love comes and loves go,

Love has memories of friends

You will never forget from above

So, talk to someone

Please don't try what I *once* almost did

Don't keep it bottled inside,

Talk to someone, because you are not alone

Look At Thyself

Judge me now, for you will be judged later

Not by me, but by our Father

You may dislike me, and categorize me

if you so please, for reasons of your own will of my deeds

I have to face *our* Father for my own

and you for yours, instead of worrying of me

worry for thyself

for yours may be deeper

than the dislike from you of my own

Remove the bandages

There is something

we try to forget push out of our lives

most of the time

it is something for which we use bandages

to cover the scars of that pain

but we need to take it and hold on

and mature from it all

This something is OUR past

Remove the bandages and learn from it

Time

Time stands still only in your mind

time keeps moving every second

every minute of the hour

Our mistakes are that we hold on to the past

which makes time stand still, only in our mind

But you have to let it go

in order to see that time keeps moving

the future is there for you

so let your time keep moving

in your mind most of all

Roses or Weeds

There are roses and there are weeds

which one are you

Roses, are sweet smelling, rich in color

and pretty to see assuming the exterior

meaning, nice, gracious, smart and unique

Weeds, are straggly, wild and dull to see

assuming the exterior meaning, evil, boisterous

not smart but still unique

Is this true, do you think or are looks deceiving

Roses are weeds, and weeds are roses

sometimes

don't you think

Dear Friend

Friendship is love

Love is friendship

to have someone in your life

That cares enough to listen

Learn, and understand you

You are my dear and beloved friend

Of all aspects

Always enlighten me with a smile

Keep me smiling and I will keep

That same smile on your face

Forever

Love,

Your Friend

Resurrection

Always destruction and no resurrection

I am just a woman

Seeking a man to build and live

What is it, do you love me

Do you want me?

It hurts not be loved by the one you love

Destruction falls in my lap at all times

Can there be some resurrection

What is it that I am doing wrong?

What are you doing wrong?

I cannot see from the destruction over again

Can I have some resurrection?

Wish that you could see that I am all you get

No more, just me

Is it not enough?

Seems as if you are seeking other resurrection

This might always end up in destruction

Then attempt to come back and try resurrection

Then it is too late because the love is not the same

I was building *alone* before, and once again, there is

destruction

Can there EVER be some resurrection

Woman and Man

When the time comes

You will praise my name

Until then, you only blame

And shame

I try to abide by your mankind

Until I do, you have to

Praise my name

I am a woman, of respect and class

No one like me, no one can be like me

I am unique, and only here to please

Please my desires and bless your needs

When the time comes

I will get that respect, of the upper class

No one will surpass the goodness of my class

Take heed and listen to my plea

For when the time comes

You will praise my name

I see a man, as a person of the test

Test of time, test of faith

My expectations of you are high

Unfortunately, you make them fall behind

So now my expectations of a man

Are sort of low, so the test of time

Is still in effect

However, when the time comes

You will praise my name

Because the test of faith

Has almost, gone to shame

Unique I am

Someone once said to me

That I would never be on there level

They were wrong

You see I am alive and I am free

I am unique in my own way

Just because you may perceive to be classy

Materialistically with an attitude

Does not mean you are

I have my classiness from the heart

Therefore, it is real, unlike a dream

I like her style

He says, but her style is false

Why do you admire a phony hype?

A natural real down to earth style

Is the true key

Fronting is not my game being real is what I am

My heart is like a diamond

its fine, shiny, see the rainbow

It is forever

When cut into pieces, cannot put back together

Therefore, my style is unique

It only comes in a few *shapes*, and *sizes*

About Me

Just as you see me

Unable to touch my soul

Able to touch my heart

Never a friend to leave you alone

Inner self is what I reach to proclaim

Taking it all

Answering only to my name

Beauty is always a part of me

Even better coming from my family tree

Tasteful

Thankful

Strong and always standing

Never will I be alone

No Different

I sat and watched how people looked

at other people, who may have been less fortunate than the

but just because that person has no home

does not mean you are better than he is

You may have a home to sleep at night

and he may have a hole to sleep for the night

still does not mean you are better than he is

He may rumble through garbage to feed himself

and you go home and cook dinner for the night

still don't mean you are better than he is

You may have a job you work to be paid

and he may collect bottles to be paid

he may even beg, just to have a nickel or two

Who is to say you are better than he is

He is a man, and you say you are too

so why not help if you feel you are better than he is

Don't be a fool

I saw this couple pushing a stroller with belongings

I wonder what happened to make them fall about

This world is hard but to lose what you have

is easier than holding on to your bed at night

You can never say, this will not happen to you

for if you do, you are a fool with no clue

I have been down and almost out

but I stood my ground and borrowed no doubt

Something you really do not want to do

because your pride can make you and break you too

You have to keep trying until you win

because success in life

is more than power or even a dollar bill

A Mans World

The DIVINE, extremist of my own needs

Involving only that come with a need

Many may want to be a part of me

Only to see what they can achieve

This is my life, I choose as I please

Holding my head high

Above the WORLD to succeed

Yes, I am a man of many dreams

So when you step into my world

All of the above

You will see the will of my deed

Eventually, my life will succeed of this test

Zeroing in on MY DESTINY of the, optimist

I am who I am

Some will say I am the MOON

how they see me is not all true

Alternately, I am the SUN

rising in the sky on a clear summer day

Only to brighten so you can feel my mood

never to let anyone be so cruel

Most of all

it isn't hard to say ever so sweet and full of play

roaming and reaching to catch the sky...

hoping and praying to keep hope alive

Anyone will see that I am but...

Meek

Needless to say take me as you see fit

for GOD

I only care to satisfy my need

4
Dreams

Dream of my man

When I lay down at night, I think of you

Even though you are not next to me

I think of you to say Goodnight

When I awake in the morning, I think of you

Even though you are still not there

Just to say, good morning my love

During the day I think of you to say hello

How is your day?

They working you too hard

I am going to beat them up

Joking, of course

You open your lunch and there is a little note

That says, I have something waiting for you later

You smile and say, oh she so sweet

However, I did not make your lunch

I think of you coming home and greet you

At the door with a kiss, a smile, not a frown after a hard day

I cook you a beautiful dinner with a note under your napkin

that says, "I love you"

Its bedtime, we caress, we talk, and we cuddle

Once again, you are not next to me

When I lay down to dream

Love to me is

A warm feeling flowing through your veins

Not just words of lust

Lusting for someone is not love

It is a fragment of your imagination

Many fail to realize that

When you love someone

You want to be with that person

You desire that person

Want to protect and support that person

You want to satisfy that person with all you got

I love you, easily said

Being in love is even harder to say

Because it's a deep feeling coming from within

From within your soul

Nature of Love

Looking over the lake

Watching the ducks make ripples in the water

Such a nice sight to see

The mountain of trees with birds flying over

Soft summer breeze

Soft fall breeze

A sight I would love to watch

With the love of my dreams

Finally

When we kiss its like fire

I feel warmth through my body

A feeling I longed for so long

When you touch me

I feel warmth from your touch

When I look into your eyes

I see a bright shining star

When I see your face

I see a rainbow

When we hold each other

Close we become one

I think I *finally* found that pot of Gold

An Angel

One day I awaken and saw the sun

it was shining so bright and sky so blue

for an early morning so new

However, it was not the sun, it was my heart

it was full of love, desire and excitement

I looked in the mirror and there was a glow

a glow from which I never seen before

I reached to stretch from a feeling so odd

a feeling of a presence I could not recognize

As I stretched I looked, looked in the mirror

there were wings behind me, which lighten the room

While, I stood there looking I realized the mood

I was an *Angel*...

Imagination

Have you ever sat and watched the clouds

on a nice clear summer day

If you're in the south you can see them

oh so clear fluffy and white, make a shape

or two, go ahead, its not hard

Just imagine once again as if you were a kid

it's a feeling you can learn to endure once again

I can imagine and I can see all sorts of shapes

so clear, don't ever let that fade from you

just keep watching the clouds and let your

imagination shine, all the way through

The Light

Standing in a crowd

With people all around

So much darkness in such a large crowd

A light shining down

But only on me

Oh, I looked around to see

If any other, light was shining on another

Oh, so much darkness

All around, no other light except

Shining on me

SA

I received these flowers

but who sent them, just a card that said

"your eyes are like the brightest of stars

your heart is filled with righteous

your smile is like a halo in the sky

Hope this will brighten your day

Take care from your SA"

At the time, I thought SA meant secret admirer

but one day, I found out it meant

from your *"Salvation of Angels"*

The Day of the Flowers

One day on the ferry, with the sun

glistening, and the clam breeze blowing

relaxing and enjoying the ride home, for the weekend

So many people with expressions of all sorts

Except this one lady, in the section I was in

as she walked by, she had the most beautiful flowers

someone had given to her that day

She walked with confidence, and love in her heart

Such a gesture for someone to think of her that way

One day, I want to receive flowers as such

from someone who thinks of me that way

Don't wait until I am gone

give them to me now, so I can see

smell and touch them

for when I am gone I can do neither

5
Life

Overcome

Living and loving'

Loving and living'

Reaching and striving

Obama, King, Malcolm

Dreams were and now are

Living and loving'

Loving and living'

Once wasn't now we are

We always was

But others thought wasn't

Truth always comes

Now its here

Living and loving'

Loving and living'

Wanting and desiring

We have overcome

Our dreams are living

Getting to know me

You try to pick my brain

However, you do not know me

You ask me questions

However, you cannot get to know me that way

My answers may not be quite accurate

Because I don't know you

Not that I am lying to you

Just watching my steps of giving too much information

Too much information too soon

Could be detrimental

I want to know you and picking your brain is not my way

I listen to all you say

And dissect it later if not then

I watch your actions in all you do

If you say you are calling or coming through

And you don't that is getting to know you

Not necessarily so in a negative way

Just getting to know your flaws to a point

However, all is ok because we are not faultless

Want to know me, be with me, and learn me

Endure me, love me, and appreciate me

Respect me, and I will show and give you all you need to know

Poem from the heart

All the days of my life

Since I got out on my own

Even a few years before that mode

Experiences in life dealt to me

Have been good and bad

We go through these things

This really is too sad

However, all it takes is a strong heart

And a strong mind

To take it all in stride

Just keep moving

Cause there is no place to hide

It all comes out, through darkness comes light

This brings happiness to your life

Your Seed

The sweet flower essence of her smile

She gives when you look into her eyes

I could never, leave that smile

Let another steal that away

She is young, she is sweet, and she is very meek

Young and fragile to the bone

Very bright, so we know

Her name is part of me, part of you

There is no other but GOD himself

That could take her away from us

No man, no woman is worth the smile I get in the morning

The kiss I get during the day

The hugs I get all day

And to hear I love you

On any given day

I love my baby to the core

She deserves a loving, giving, trusting

Honest Mommy and Daddy role model for her future

So her sweet flower smile can say, when I get big

I want a husband like my daddy, and *love* like my mommy

Isn't that a sweet thing to say from a flower smile of your very

Own essence

Mother

Mother of all mothers

You strive to make all things right

Even when you know, you cannot

God has blessed you with this gift that you have

You are a saint, in your own way

You are *phenomenal*

Phenomenal woman you are

Your love is in abundance

And abundance, which cures our pain

Kiss the boo-boo and heal the heart

We love you mommy

Forever and a day

Father

The opportunity to know you is a blessing

Knowing you teaches me who I am

Why I am, who I be

You are I, and I am you

When I was a child, I wondered who I was

Not like whom I thought was

Now this explains why

I love it

With learning to love you the same

My father, my life

Thank you for my life

Wish you were in it earlier

Later is just as good

Happy 1st Father's Day, *Daddy*

Sisters

My blood, my sibling my life beyond my life

you are a part of me, may even look like me

we've had some hard times while growing up

even a fight or two, but you are still my sister day and night

We have shared and we have cried

When one hurts, the other even feels the pain

Even though we are growing up and growing a far

does not mean you are not my sister

and I am saying this in vain

Our mother bared us and so did father

but mother was always there, even when father went away

We are part of both of them

but mostly of our mother dear

You are my sister and it is so very clear

that I will always love you to the *very end*

Brother

Brother I never had

Brother I do not know

Wish I knew you or had you to protect me

To teach me things to be aware of

Things happen in our lives that we did not ask for, placed

upon us

Therefore, we take it as we see fit

Male cousins were my brothers

Nevertheless, it is not the same

Brother of mine, Brother could have been

Wish I had known you

Maybe I would have understood more

More or just did things differently

But neither here nor there

Learning experiences

Have proved me right and wrong

Brother, wish to know you

From your daughter

Keep me safe, from all who do not care

everyone who cares, will love me dear

You are my Mommy and my Daddy

only love me for being me

Never to leave me by myself

inside and out we will always be

Love is near and never far

you are my life, no matter where we are

Nobody knows the true love I receive

note this for the future tree

Ready and waiting to be a lady

on my knees I pray to thee

GOD be with me on my way

extreme love of life, I will achieve

Ready and able to ALWAYS succeed for

Sweetness, is all I will be

Dear Mama

I thank you for raising me with morals

Principles and respect

You did your best for all of us

I may have given you grief here and there

Oh, thinking I knew so much

Now, I am a mother

I see what I put you through

I know it is a phase and she will be saying

The same thing to me one day

For if she does

I know I raised her well

Thank you my teacher, teacher of life

Dear Mama

He's there

When I lost most of it all

I thought to myself

Oh, what have I done?

Then someone said to me

Do not fret, because God is there

Just reach out and grab his hand

He will lead you on your way

I was still scared of losing more

However, I kept God in my sight

Pieces came together little by little

Now I am almost where I once was

Determined to be more than what I was

Joy vs. Pain

The first three months

Feeling woozy and sick

When the next three months

you feel like turning flips

the last three months feeling stuffed you see

but when its time, its time when that pain comes in

It is like no other pain, no pain to describe

you remember but to describe it is not so kind

You push, and you push

Oh, so much pain, but to hear that cry

Will put a smile on your face

The joy from that delicate life you bore

makes you forget all the pain, from before

Going Home

Something we all have to face

oh, we do not want to, reality we know it is at our pace

Live your life day by day, and do all that you can

We all are God's children he gave us breath and one day

he calls us back and our breath is taken away

Only to endure the better side of this all

to be in his presence will be the best of all

No pain, no sorrow no sadness to see

The opening of the pearly gates is where I want to be

When my gracious God take my breath away

Therefore, I can go home to stay

Life

Life is what you make of it

Use every chance to survive

At a high, medium or low level

One important thing is

Be decent and sincere

Have self-confidence you can do anything

Anything you put your heart and mind to

You see, your heart has to be in it

Not only in your mind

That is only touching the surface

And wasting nothing but time

Deep in the core of life is what we are striving to survive

So always keep God first and take his hand

Let him lead you and continue to strive

Let it go

Sometimes in life, we are afraid of change

Afraid to let things go

Afraid that change is not good

Sometimes when there are breakups

The pain is so ruthless it feels only bad can come from it

Sometimes we need to grasp that change

Even if we do not want to, because there is a reason for

everything

Could mean you require this separation

To see if you really love each other

To understand what you really had

Maybe the separation is destined to be

Maybe to teach a lesson, even to others

Sometimes we get hurt in that process of

teaching others, to make room for changes in your life

their life, so receive it, stop trying to hold on

Just let it go

The pain is going to be there

It *will* get easier

If he or she *really* loves you, *maybe* they will return

If it's not too *late*

But whatever the case, even when we do not agree

Change is going to happen because life is unpredictable

Thanks and Advisement

Thank you, and keep an eye out for more books from Author,

Juanita Betts.

Leaving you with this message:::

Love is a gift from GOD; he loved us first and gave us a gift to

love and always keep him first. We have this ONE LIFE, so use it

wisely. If you want something make an effort and use what you

have to get what you want, but respect yourself and keep your

dignity.

Do not settle for less than what you want, no matter what, claim

your worth, and always, Love You More.

God Bless, be CONFIDENT in your own skin,

and let your life prosper!

Thank You